YOUR KNOWLEDGE HAS VALUE

Cyril Alias

Transport policy in Europe

Concepts and objectives for a sustainable transport system

GRIN Verlag

Bibliografische Information der Deutschen Nationalbibliothek:

Die Deutsche Bibliothek verzeichnet diese Publikation in der Deutschen National-
bibliografie; detaillierte bibliografische Daten sind im Internet über http://dnb.d-
nb.de/ abrufbar.

Imprint:

Copyright © 2008 GRIN Verlag GmbH
Druck und Bindung: Books on Demand GmbH, Norderstedt Germany
ISBN: 978-3-638-93926-3

This book at GRIN:

http://www.grin.com/en/e-book/89965/transport-policy-in-europe

University of Duisburg and Essen (Campus Duisburg)
Department of Biology and Geography
Institute of Geography (Economic Geography, Transports and Logistics)
Transports and Sustainability
Winter Term 2007/08

Transport policy in Europe

Concepts and objectives for a sustainable transport system

Table of contents

I. Introduction

All over the history, mobility has been an integral part of life. Europe features a high level of its unmatched infrastructure, allowing that mobility very well. Not only mobility of people, also the conveyance of goods profits from it. It has become a part of the European lifestyle since the citizens of the continent make use of transport services as a matter of course. Although the term 'Europe' is used, the essay mainly contains remarks about the transport sector of the European Union with its 27 member states by now.

Today, transportation can be described as one of those sectors which have been impacted most by the general change of our times. The massive growth of certain modes of transport in the past 50 years and the progression of ever increasing passengers and goods traffic constitute this change. Liberalisation, intensified competition and internationalised services in a common Internal Market emerged as results of the same.

However, there exist perils of the sector reaching its limits since new challenges occur at the horizon. In the wake of expanding trade relations and of globalisation in general, a soaring volume of goods carriers is said to overwhelm and, sooner or later, also to overtax European roads and rails. Slight changes in lifestyle patterns towards more mobility, esp. regarding everyday moves, leisure trips and vacation times, also add to the problem by creating even more traffic. Growing concern is added by the recent EU- or worldwide concentration on topics of climate change, emissions and noise pollution as well as rising number of traffic deaths and increased ground sealing by ever new projects, all of which would possibly lead to a fatal incapability of action for the sector. Another issue is the dependency on imports of (fossil) fuels which already has proved to limit the political leeway of the Union in order to placate energy supplying countries and their politicians. Likewise, the skyrocketing of crude oil prices can turn out to be a problem.

Sustainable transport should address these problems without constraining the benefits of the good infrastructure. Therefore, it is the current key trend of the European transport sector.

In this essay, the objectives of the European governmental bodies in Brussels in order to develop a sustainable transport system in the Union will be presented, so will the concepts and technologies to be applied. Included in the concepts are environmental and social considerations, providing for the observation of the sustainability idea without sacrificing economic and political objectives of the Union. In order to grasp the recommendations from Brussels thoroughly, the status quo of the sector and the different modes should be made aware of first.

II. Definitions

Transportation is termed as "the totality of all translocations of persons [...] and goods [...] as well as news [...]" (from: Meyers1 2007), "which is to be geared to the needs for activity of men and to the environment." (from: Ammoser/Hoppe 2006)
The transport sector comprehends the extent of passenger use, the frequency of the lanes, the usage of the different means of transportation and the covered distances. (cp. Ammoser/Hoppe 2006; Meyers1 2007)

Transport policy can be understood as "a governmental [and public] field of responsibility, which refers to the general existence provision, pursuing the goals of planning and implementing the transport infrastructure anticipatorily, of coordinating and controlling the use of transport ways and of enabling economically [i.e. cost] efficient, ecologically compatible and socially well-balanced transportation." (from: Nuhn/Hesse 2006)
As for the transport policy in the member states of the European Union, there exists a supranational level in Brussels, apart from the respective national, regional and communal levels. Likewise, economic, financial and research policies interact with the transport policy. (cp. Meyers2 2007)

Sustainability is defined as "the state of a development, which satisfies the need for the presence without threatening the ability of future generations to satisfy their very own needs as well" (from: Brundtland 1987; cp. Meyers3 2007). In terms of sustainability in transportation, three main strategies can be identified: traffic prevention, modal shift and the increase of efficiency and compatibility. Yet, these strategies can only be realized simultaneously when an integrated transportation management is in use. (cp. DIB 2000)

A *White Paper* is often the second communicative measure of the European Commission in a in a legislation process of the European Union. (cp. Eurordis 2007) Prior to it, a so-called Green Paper is produced, containing rather general ideas or questions pertaining to a problem or issue and aiming at both "holding discussions with the European civil society [...] [and paving] the way towards the drafting of a Commission proposal" (from: Eurordis 2007). So, normally Green Papers try to launch the public discussion which eventually culminates in the afore-mentioned Commission proposal.

Then, as a following step, the White Paper already contains "the main guidelines of a legislative proposal" (from: Eurordis 2007), i.e. it can be seen as the concrete (intermediate) result of the public discussion. Derived from the White Paper, certain concrete laws on national or Union level can be initiated.

III. The transport sector of the European Union

As the title of this essay indicates, it is to deal with the concepts and objectives of a common transport policy throughout the European Union.

The central and decisive element in this matter is the White Paper 'European transport policy for 2010 – Time to decide', published at the Gothenburg European Council in 2001. This document contains the essential abstract objectives and concrete measures or concepts for a more sustainable transport policy across the Union territory. These goals and measures can roughly be assigned to the two main categories of performance-enhancement and climate protection.

In the following, the present essay aims at pointing out both objectives and measures. However, in order to be capable of understanding the White Paper properly and thoroughly, it is important to conceive the origin it stems from. For that reason, the historical development of the policy shall be introduced at first, before viewing the status quo on the European transport systems. In the consideration of the present situation, a particular emphasis is laid on the state of the different modes of transport and on the current modal split.

In the light of both considerations, the White Paper is going to be introduced. As mentioned before, the White Paper already comprises legislative suggestions and distinct measures, next to abstract visions and objectives underlying these. The Commission document is subdivided into four different parts or policy guidelines, each of which pursues another goal. To each part, several measures are mentioned answering the questions what the respective issue to be tackled actually is and how the given objective can be fulfilled in an appropriate and timely manner. An important building block among those measures is the introduction of so-called Trans-European Networks, which will shortly be introduced in a later section. Moreover, their role in the framework of a common, Union-wide policy shall be examined. Furthermore, the various obstacles awaited by the European Commission are to be introduced as well.

Finally, the interim results are to be presented shortly along with future prospects, taking the enlargement rounds of the Union in 2004 and 2007 into account.

1. The history of the European transport policy

In the 'Treaty establishing the European Union'[1], the Article 3f[2] and Title V[3] (ECB 2007; EurActiv1 2006) build the basis for a common European transport policy.

Yet, this has merely been in charge for one and a half decades now. The ambitions exist far longer though.

In 1957, the Treaty of Rome was signed by the six member states of the European Economic Community, which was established with the treaty. In the latter, a separate section[4] had been dedicated to the need of a harmonized transport infrastructure in the way that measures were to be taken which were common and coordinated with each other. Modernisation, on the one hand, and extension of the existing infrastructure posed the main focus of the time, both aiming at the provision of the best conditions for an economic boom in post-war Europe. (cp. Weidenfeld 1992, pp. 14, 15; cp. Button 1992, pp. 44 - 54)

However, these two ambitions largely stayed dull theory since other fields, such as the Common Agricultural Policy, pulled the political attention towards them. Moreover, the willingness to deregulate the national transport markets was quite low due to different competitive conditions in the member states. (cp. Button 1992, pp. 14, 15; cp. Towey 2005)

During the 1960s, the European Commission recommended the establishment of a transportation network in order to safeguard the economic operability in the Community. Concrete coordinated activities were lacking though. (cp. Button 1992, pp. 14 - 17)

In the following years, the growth in the transport sector, increasingly massive in extent and complex in nature, began. As for passenger transport, the growth encompassed all modes of transportation, the road sector even well above average. Similarly, the freight transportation also experienced a huge surge in the past three and a half decades. This increase was mainly absorbed by the road sector all alone, accepted by the European Commission, while railway and inland waterways remained at their respective (absolute) values of the early 1970s. (cp. ECMT 2005, pp. 22, 32, 49 - 53, 55 - 59)

Questions regarding the financing of and the responsibilities during transport extension or modernisation projects still appeared on the agenda. Yet, despite

---

[1] Treaty of Maastricht.
[2] As a part of the Economic and Monetary Union, a "common policy in the sphere of transport" shall be pursued. (from: Eur-Lex n.d.)
[3] Common rules on competition, taxation and approximation of laws
[4] Title IV of the Treaty of Rome deals with the topic of transport explicitly

standing in the face of this dynamic developments, a coordinated approach throughout the European Community has been absent for long, for which again both infrastructural and regulatory assimilation would have been necessary. Aside from the many rather half-hearted notices of intent, comprehensive measures were missing. (cp. Button 1992, pp. 17, 43)

In 1985, when the economic growth has been in place for several years and the then-existing transport system came to its limits, the European Parliament filed a suit against the European Council at the European Court of Justice in Luxembourg due to failure to act. The claim was admitted and the European Council correspondingly released new impulses. (cp. Braun-Moser 1989, pp. 9 - 11; cp. Button 1992, pp. 15, 40, 41; cp. Towey 2005)

Immediately after the Court decision has the European Commission published a White Paper containing the legal proposals for the completion of the Internal Market and, with these, the advice for liberalisation and harmonization of the transport policy of the Community. (cp. EurActiv1 2006; cp. Mehl 2004, pp. 42 - 44) This document showed signs of having triggered some acceleration of the process since first cross-border cooperation projects, or such with more than one interested party involved or affected, were to be gone about. (cp. Braun-Moser 1989, pp. 9 – 11; cp. Button 1992, pp. 15, 44)

In the 1990s, several Green Papers, White Papers, notices and other forms of stimuli regarding the transport sector have been issued by the European Union. (cp. EurActiv1 2006; cp. EU-Hist1 n.d.) In 1992, the first White Paper explicitly dealing with the transport sector has been published, which was recommending the further "opening-up of the transport market" (from: EU-WP 2001, p. 10) for European competition. In the same year, the Maastricht Treaty, including "the principle of the need to develop the TENS" (from: Towey 2005) in order to achieve the goals set, was signed. (cp. EU-Hist1 n.d.; cp. EU-WP 2001, pp. 10, 11; cp. Towey 2005) Likewise, "the political, institutional and budgetary foundations for transport policy" (from: EU-WP 2001, p. 10) were laid. In the consecutive year, the completion of the Internal Market has been finalized with effects on the transport sector. (cp. EU-Hist3 n.d.) For instance, the acts concerning Free Movement of Persons and of Goods led to a further boost of cross-national passenger and freight transport.

In 1994, during a European Council in Essen, Germany, the necessity of a transportation network was remembered. The so-called 'Essen List' in 1996 with fourteen priority transport infrastructure projects covering all Europe was the outcome there. Again, the ultimate goal lay in economic growth and the enhancement of prosperity. (cp. EurActiv1 2006; cp. EU-Hist4 n.d.) So, until the mid-1990s the general perception implied a proportional relation between the extent of transport infrastructure and economic well-being.

The Treaty of Amsterdam from 1997 deals with the reforms needed in the light upcoming enlargement of the European Union, amongst other topics. As regards the transport market, enabling performance and further liberalization were the main points on the agenda, predominantly to invigorate the regulations for the Internal Market. (cp. EU-Hist5 n.d.)

In the following year, another White Paper has been brought out, addressing the possible legal conditions for tolls for infrastructure use. (cp. EurActiv1 2006) Although not appearing that noteworthy, this is a substantial shift in the mentality within the organisation of the European Union: The necessity of a more sensible and responsible exposure to infrastructure use and transportation in general has been seen. By charging tolls, the demand should be constrained. But this was not accompanied by an abdication of economic ambitions, not even a reduction. But, since then, the objective of uncoupling economic growth from infrastructural compaction stood in the centre of all considerations in this matter. Sustainability occurred as a core element in transport planning. This does not mean that the goals have actively been pursued, merely the intention had been uttered. The Lisbon strategy with the core objectives 'growth' and 'employment' was said not to be inconsistent with the new sustainability focus in the transport sector. Quite the contrary, it has even been identified as a crucial catalyst for the Lisbon process, in view of the plenty of room for optimisation in terms of emissions and energy consumption. (cp. BMVBS3 2007, p. 6)

Consequently, a new White Paper with the name 'European transport policy for 2010 – Time to decide' has been launched in 2001, which is going to be introduced in detail at a later stage of this essay. As a short prospect though, it can be regarded as the centre of today's European transport policy and it deals with the sustainability idea, covering the dimensions of economy, society and ecology. In detail, the international politics and economy, the infrastructural requirements and the domestic developments, i.e. user-focused changes and the ones related to the transport modes, are under discussion in the document. It has to do both with safeguarding the capability of enabling high (economic) performance and with promoting eco-friendly technologies and lifestyles. (cp. EU-Got 2001, pp. 3, 4; cp. EU-WP 2001, pp. 10 - 21; cp. EurActiv1 2006)

Since the White Paper directed to a period until 2010, a mid-term review of the objectives and the process of achieving the latter seemed to be sensible because many historical steps in common European history, namely primarily the eastern enlargement and, thus, the overcoming of a decade-old east-west-division of the continent, have taken place in the meantime. The corresponding report, launched in 2006, underwent some amendments and corrections in order to make the reform of the transport sector more appropriate to the real needs of the inhabitants of the Union. (cp. EurActiv1 2006) This mid-term review will be examined later as well.

To the most recent 'jigsaw pieces' in the long story belongs a Green Paper from September 2007 with the title 'Towards a new culture for urban mobility', dealing with issues of urban transportation. Actually, parts of the content of this document can be seen as a derivation of the 2001 White Paper into a smaller, i.e. urban, setting. So, the White Paper can be considered as a mastermind piece for the transport-related legislation in the coming years.

Having seen the major milestones of the past of a common European transport policy, the next field of attention is the present, the status quo in Europe's transport infrastructure.

2. Status quo of the transport sector in the Union

For the status quo, three sections are to be mentioned in particular: The general state of the different modes of transport as well as the modal split in the Union will be presented in the following subchapter. Afterwards, resulting from the present modal split situation, the various problems haunting the road, rail, aviation and water-borne transport sector are the subject matters of the following sections.

1. The various modes of transportation and the modal split

To start with the present state of the European transport sector, the general growth will be presented at first. Between 1995 and 2004, the goods traffic in Europe grew by 2.8% p.a., making a total increase of 28%, whereas in the same period the passenger transportation experienced an annual increase of 1.8%, leading to 18% in total. The rates grossly correspond to the average yearly economic growth of 2.3%. (cp. EU-TPO 2006, p. 10)

So, a clear connection between economic growth (the rate predicted for the time between 2000 and 2020 account for 2.1% p.a. and 52% in total) and the increase of traffic volume still cannot be dismissed. Considering the predicted total growth of over 50% in goods conveyance and over 35% in passenger traffic until 2020, the necessity for the envisaged uncoupling of the economic growth from the increase in traffic volume is highly visible. (cp. EU-TPO 2006, p. 11)

However, the growth hitherto is not evenly distributed onto the different transport modes at all. While the road sector and the short-sea sector have both grown by 35% (goods) and 17% (passengers) respectively each, the situation is rather devastating for inland waterways and railways. The railways' share has even suffered a dramatic decline in the elapsed half century, while inland water transport has not managed to raise its prevalence in the Union. The outstanding performer among the various transport modes is the aviation sector though, with a growth of above 50% between 1995 and 2004, which but is largely referring to the passenger transport range. (cp. EU-TPO 2006, p. 10)

Currently, the modal split situation for the goods conveyance sector presents itself as follows: The major sectors accommodate more than four fifth of the total extent, with the road sector holding 44% and the sea another 39%. A tenth can be credited to the railways' account while the balance is nearly evenly spread on inland waterways with 4% and pipelines with 3%. Air cargo transports are merely represent with 0.1% and can hence be neglected in the further consideration.[5] (cp. EU-Road 2007, p. 2; cp. EU-TPO 2006, pp. 10, 11, 39)

The strength of the road sector, i.e. the more comprehensive road network in comparison with other modes, basically has to do with the structural preference for this sector in the past, as has been outlined in the previous chapter. Apart from that, the prevailing trends currently point at general cargo haulage and at optimised services emphasizing punctuality and convenience to the customer, such as 'just-in-time' and 'door-to-door' offers.

Since "two thirds of [the Union] boundaries [are] facing the sea" (from: EU-TPO 2006, p. 15) and "nearly 90% of the external trade" (from: EU-TPO 2006, p. 11) of the European Union is conducted by means of vessel assistance, the prevalence of

---

[5] Please see annex, figure 1.

water-borne transportation in the EU may not appear that surprising. The dynamics of the sector indicates its significance and the recency of this development. However, the difference between shipments related to external trade, which is mostly handled by sea nowadays, and shipments between the member states, where alternative modes dominate the market. Since not all member states are endued with great waterways, the acceptance of inland waterways varies largely between the regions and eventually is low in EU average. This vast hidden potential in many countries can (and possibly must) be exploited in the coming years.

The rail sector suffers from a decline lasting for nearly a half century now. Latterly, the trend could be cushioned and sporadically even reversed. The reasons for the poor performance of the rail segment will be discussed more in detail at a later stage.

With regard to the distribution of the quantity of passenger carriage to the different modes, the following result can be presented: The dominance of the road sector is even more evident, with an outstanding share of 84% being allotted to cars as well as busses and coaches. Next follows air transport with 8% before railways with 7% (including trains, metros and trams). The residual percentage point is allotted to sea transportation, i.e. ferries and similar means of travel.[6] (cp. EU-Road 2007, p. 2; cp. EU-TPO 2006, pp. 10, 11, 39)

While the road sector again profits from the well developed network built in the past decades throughout the Union territory, additional arguments for the popularity of this mode can be found in the alleged lack of flexibility and convenience (esp. for short and medium distances) of other modes, yet also in lifestyle and prestige reasons.

In the light of the constant decline over the elapsed decades, it can be made a note of the conclusion that the railway sector has, at least so far, failed to build itself up as a key mode in passenger transportation. Merely, a flicker of hope comes along with the introduction of few high-speed train connections covering long distances across Europe. (cp. EU-Rail 2003, p. 5; cp. Max-Planck 1987, p. 25)

Having overtaken railways on rank two by now, the aviation sector is the main mode for long distance passenger transportation due to its speed, convenience, and cost-efficiency. More than a quarter of the sector's performance within the Union falls upon low-cost carriers, which also have fuelled the growth of regional airports and, thus, created a denser network. (cp. EU-Air 2007, p. 5; cp. EU-TPO 2006, pp. 12, 15, 16)

---

[6]   Please see annex, figure 1.

2.   The situation and challenges for transports over Europe's roads

Being the main transport mode with 4.5 million jobs and constituting 1.6% of the GDP in the EU, the road sector, meanwhile traditionally, takes a central role in the Union's transport policy. Lying at 19.7% in 1960, the share of road-borne transportation has constantly developed upwards to 34.6% in 1970, 41.8% in 1990 and 44.4% in 2005.[7] (cp. EU-Rail 2003, p. 2; cp. EU-Road 2007, p. 2; cp. Max-Planck 1987, p. 25)

The appreciation is due to the fact that it is the only mode which can safeguard punctuality, reliability and convenience simultaneously. Therefore, a lorry oftentimes stands at the beginning and the very end of a logistical chain. The strong position of the mode is the result of continuous promotion over the past years and decades. In addition, globalisation and growing adhesion among the member states have led to a considerable multiplication of traffic volume, both in the passenger and in the goods field. The extension of the road network is still not of highest priority in the coming years, despite some urgent projects in the new member states and some major international axes. (cp. EU-Road 2007, pp. 2, 3, 11, 12)

Additional growth of the sector, which might be inevitable in order to meet the goals of the Lisbon agenda, can be expected with further liberalization measures by which the access of new companies and new services onto the European road transport market are to be alleviated. As a result, more and more high-class services for lower costs can be expected.

As an example for a field to be liberalized, cabotages can be mentioned. Cabotages are transport services carried out in a country by a foreign haulage company. They should be allowed not merely on a temporary basis, as it happens at the moment. However, services that are already largely liberalized, such as cross-border transportation, are inducing very beneficial effects to the participating parties. On the whole, the support of the Internal Market integration, i.e. mainly the Free Movement of Persons and Goods, should stand in the centre of future decisions. Yet, some adjustments, e.g. the harmonisation of vehicle and fuel taxation differing from member state to member state, are pending but decisive for the acceptance of the liberalization since only with a common legislation can competitive inequalities be banned. (cp. EU-Road 2007, pp. 2 - 5, 10, 11; cp. EU-TPO 2006, p. 13; cp. Mehl 2004, pp. 42 - 50)

As has been mentioned before, a long-term uncoupling of economic growth from traffic volume increase has to be purposed in today's decision-making processes

---

[7]   Please see annex, figure 2.

14

though. Having said that, it is equally important not to exaggerate the containment of the volume increase and, thereby, to choke off the growth and job creation impulses required by the Lisbon strategy. (cp. EU-Road 2007, p. 4)

A first step in the direction of an uncoupling of economic and traffic growth is a new emphasis to be placed on efficiency, safety and cost-efficiency. Charging for infrastructure use partly already is and, in future, will even more be an adequate measure to both raise the efficiency of the network and to internalise external costs arising from the use. Even a change in lifestyle patterns might be hoped for. Besides, new financing schemes might relieve the pressure on public authorities to raise funds sufficiently and timely. (cp. EU-Road 2007, pp. 2, 4, 10)

Efficiency can be raised in more than merely this way though. The fact that, up to this very day, a quarter of all lorries all over the Union territory run empty, has a negative financial impact on the companies concerned and, thus, their customers. Congestion is another huge problem, both for passenger and goods conveyance. Needless to say, these lacks of efficiency also cause harmful environmental and ecological consequences with a quarter of the entire energy consumption in the Union falling upon this mode. At the same time, accessibility of remote areas in the Union is a problem as there exist too few powerful links.

Another negative impact of the extensive use of the road network is high number of road fatalities and the security concerns involved. Actually, the vast majority of traffic-related death cases are caused by road accidents. (cp. ECMT 2005, pp. 38 - 45, 61 - 63; cp. EU-Road 2007, pp. 3, 6 – 9; cp. EU-TPO 2006, p. 35; cp. EuroStat10 n.d.)

3. The situation and challenges for conveyance via European railways

Currently, the railway sector cannot be named a key mode in Europe with merely 10% of freight transports and 5.8%[8] of passenger transport run on rail tracks. (cp. EU-TPO 2006, p. 37) In the United States, on average every two out of five transports are carried out with assistance of the US railway sector. The potential for its European counterpart is definitely given as spare capacities and the absence of congestion would be able to indicate. History itself has already proven the strong role of European railways in the freight transport business, having induced and fuelled the economic boom in several countries of post-war Europe. (cp. Braun-Moser 1989, pp. 55, 56) Nearly half of all freight and a fifth of all passenger transports were executed with trains. (cp. Braun-Moser 1989, p. 55) In 1960, for example, the share of

---

[8]   Carriages in classic passenger trains only, metros and trams are not represented with this figure.

transports via trains lay at 44.2%. (cp. Max-Planck 1987, p. 25) Since then, a continuous decrease down to less than 6% in 2005 could be observed. (cp. EU-TPO 2006, p. 11) Little attention, few investments in the network and its maintenance and expansion and, thus, a decaying network may have been one reason for the development. Also, the general development from mass transit and mass volume transport, where the railway used to generate its effectiveness and efficiency by utilizing natural advantages, to general cargo and the demand for flexibility in modern times has led to the bad position of the mode. Another reason surely was the lack of cooperation and mutual understanding with reference to harmonisation of the partly grossly differing systems. National contemplations were regarded as more relevant than the ones at Community or Union level. (cp. Braun-Moser 1989, pp. 55 – 57; cp. EC-Rail 2007, p. 16; cp. EU-Rail 2003, pp. 2 - 10; cp. Max-Planck 1987, pp. 14, 101) The national railway markets in the EU have undergone more or less severe restructuring processes with partially dramatic cuts in workforce, but still have failed to make out the potentials to be tapped by installing a European market. Since the market shares have remained stable after the process, an expansion of the business to other EU member states, promises considerable profits, esp. with long-distance high-speed trains across the continent. (cp. EU-Rail 2003, pp. 2 - 5)

Instead, accountability discussions at national level are the rule, pertaining to service, performance as well as to managerial and financial calculations. In an international environment, the accountability of a foreign company may be noticed even clearlier as there is no leap of faith the firm can rest upon. (cp. EU-Rail 2003, pp. 5, 11) So, service quality becomes an unmistakably central criterion. Under the quality term can be pooled punctuality, speed, tracking performance and service guarantees. For example, currently goods trains are running through Europe with an average speed of 18 kilometres per hour. Too scarcely exist high-speed connections that can be used in an extensive manner. (cp. Braun-Moser 1989, pp. 57 - 61) The planned high-speed connections act therefore as the 'great white hope' of the sector, both for passenger transport and for shipment logistics, also in order to boost the acceptance of the entire mode and to halt the threat by the road sector. (cp. EU-Rail 2003, pp. 6, 10, 11; cp. EU-TPO 2006, pp. 14, 15)

Endangered is the hope by the still too fragmented rail network all over Europe, leading to a picture of a "patchwork of different rail that are not integrated or interoperable"[9] (from: EU-Rail 2003, p. 5), and of this technical incompatibility resulting in delays in international journeys, for instance.[10]

Not only are signalling, electrification and other technical differences one aspect of the impediment to growth, but also legal differences and an unequal appreciation of the respective national systems can be assigned to it. Lately, there do evolve different possible solutions, such as special locomotives for cross-national transports and diesel-electric locos for parallel use in areas without electrification. (cp. EU-Rail 2003, pp. 5, 12, 13, 22, 26)

As a qualitative downside, the problem fields mentioned here can be considered a structural barrier and destructive for the competitiveness of the entire mode, which Jacques Barrot[11] and the European Commission is aware of. (cp. EU-TPO 2006, pp. 14, 15) So, a complete reorganisation of the sector would hypothetically be preferable in order to exploit all potentials arising in the wake of a European integration. Albeit appearing very unlikely to happen immediately, certain steps into the right direction could mark a beginning, e.g. liberalization measures to promote cross-border journeys.

However, there exist far less complex quality shortcomings as well. As an example, capacities of trains and their wagons as well as their availability is not retrievable. Consequently, there is leeway upwards for capacity allocation and management in this mode. Likewise, a preferential treatment for passenger transportation compared to goods haulage can be observed in many member states, putting the situation (and the chances) of the mode in freight transport decisions within companies at a disadvantage. (cp. EU-Rail 2003, pp. 12, 13) Such practices, just as the above-mentioned negligence of investments in the network over years, again imply that not only structural obstacles, but also management errors have contributed to the inferior situation the rail mode is presently tucked in compared with the road or the sea.

As the European Commission has already contemplated, financial aid or relief could be taken in by introducing infrastructure tolls, at least for highly frequented legs. It has to be taken into consideration though that the acceptance of the mode may be entirely destroyed with such a measure. In addition, the Commission has to play the outshining climate card since railway is universally accepted as an eco-friendly and energy-efficient transport mode. Yet, the internalisation of external costs is an issue

---

[9] "Interoperability refers to a train's ability to run on any stretch of the railway network in the Union." (from: EU-Rail 2003, p. 5)

[10] Please see annex, figure 4.

[11] Current vice-president of the European Commission, responsible for transport.

in this sector as well. (cp. EU-Rail 2003, pp. 4, 6, 7, 10, 25, 27; cp. EU-TPO 2006, p. 14, 15; cp. Huber 1993, p. 50)

4.   The situation and challenges for air-borne transportation in the EU

In the wake of the well-advanced restructuring and integration processes of the aviation mode, originating from the liberalization packages of 1987 and 1993, the European Commission states that "the internal air transport market has become an industrial reality and is an engine for growth" (from: EU-TPO 2006, p. 15). Apart being an engine for growth, it has also acted as a profiteer of its own progress of increased integration. So have the customers, namely in the form of "considerable benefits" (from: EU-TPO 2006, p. 15), as the Commission confirmed. To these belong the greater choice, lower costs and better connectivity of the different regions as well as higher mobility and, thus, a lifestyle of higher value than before. At the same time, the industry profits from a more or less healthy competition and accelerated growth. (cp. Braun-Moser 1989, pp. 35 - 38; cp. EU-Air 2007, pp. 2, 3, 12)

In the mentioned action packages, new regulations (and deregulations) regarding the operational practices for internal and international flights as well as for managerial decision-making, e.g. concerning pricing, were outlined. (cp. EU-Air 2007, p. 2; cp. EU-TPO 2006, pp. 15, 16; cp. Max-Planck 1987, pp. 18, 19) To guarantee competition is the core interest of the public authorities. As visible in Figure 3[12], this goal has been achieved so far. With the growing number of carriers involved, routes served and customers satisfied, the air transport sector has laid its own fundament for the development. As an exemplification, in 2006 the number of European routes has risen to the fourfold, compared to the level of 1992.[13] (cp. EU-Air 2007, p. 5) Nowadays, the danger of congestion both on ground and in the air is set to prevail. Despite all growth, Europe has managed to keep its world-leading security and safety standards. Alongside, the 'education' of customers regarding their rights and obligations in and around aircrafts and flight journeys is another agenda item. This is necessary because the dynamic growth of the mode in the last year has let many customers lag behind in terms of dealing confidently with the industry. (cp. EU-Air 2007, pp. 3 - 5, 12)

---

[12]   Please see annex, figure 3.
[13]   Please see annex, figure 3.

Another issue in the air transport field is the difficult handling of neighbouring countries and key strategic partners[14]. Complex legislation and partly unlawful contracts under revision have led to even higher uncertainty of the situation here. The aim is the extension of the Internal Market to the neighbours and partners in order to facilitate better businesses. (cp. EU-Air 2007, pp. 5 - 11)

The Commission is aware of the fact that the "European Union is a major world player [...] in [...] aviation services" (from: EU-TPO 2006, p. 15) and that continuous improvement is essential importance to maintain the good position. Improvement means both more and better services, considering economic, social and ecological aspects. So, the dimensions of sustainability are naturally represented here, signifying that sustainable growth is also in the interests of the modal operators and stakeholders.

Naturally, globalisation has also impacted European air transports and still continues to do so. Therefore, "no time for complacency to face the challenges of continued growth and global competition" (from: EU-TPO 2006, p. 15) is allowed by the Commission. In the first instance, such challenges may refer to infrastructural bottlenecks. The capacities of airports are limited despite the recent evolvement of airports for low-cost carriers in remote areas and the well-directed construction aids from Union budgets for certain projects like the Aeroporto di Milano Malpensa in northern Italy. Further growth presupposes higher capacities both on the ground and in the air. A more efficient use of the existing capacities has also been recommended by the Commissioner, campaigning for an EU-wide air management system and related services. (cp. Braun-Moser 1989, pp. 39 - 43; cp. EU-TPO 2006, pp. 15, 16)

A substantial downside of this mode is the bad energy efficiency, i.e. the huge amounts of emissions, which have increased parallelly to the soaring growth of the mode in the past years. (cp. EU-TPO 2006, pp. 15, 16) Finding a solution for this massive problem might act as a major hindrance to further expansion and integration.

5.   The situation and challenges for the maritime transport modes in the EU

As has been pinpointed earlier, the maritime sector is of high significance in Europe. This has to do with the well-developed port network throughout the Union, esp. following the latest growth, but also with the traditional maritime imprint of European

---

[14]   For the air transport sector, the EU has identified the following countries as key partners: United States, Canada, Australia, New Zealand, Chile, PR China and India.

economy.[15] The potentials are far from fully exploited though. For many transports, it provides a genuine alternative to overloaded or inflexible modes, as the present already shows with 39% of goods transports being water-borne. (cp. EU-Mar 2006, pp. 2, 4; cp. EU-TPO 2006, pp. 16, 17) But national governments have neglected the promotion of this mode yet.

Especially in multimodal logistical chains, short-sea and long-sea shipping can play a very positive role since they can circumvent the congested road network and the poorly performing railways. Actually, multi-modal chains and the better integration of the water-based modes into the latter represent the largest prospects for further expansion. Co-modality, that means "optimally combining various modes of transport within the same transport chain" (from: EU-TPO 2006, p. 1), is more and more a modern trend since the costs from the above-mentioned problems put the operators under pressure to act. For a consistent adoption of this model, a uniform acceptance of this mode across the Union is inevitable. As has been presented earlier, this is not given as some regions rely on water transportation far more than other ones do. Additionally, cross-national traffic is still exacerbated by complicated national regulations in the various member states. A fully functioning internal sea transport market is still awaited. Not only has the Commission raised funds to promote the process actively, but it also supports the development with efforts at other ends. In order to raise performance and efficiency, the European Commissioners put their hope also in different R&D projects. (cp. EU-Mar 2006, pp. 3, 4; cp. EU-TPO 2006, pp. 16, 17; cp. Mehl 2004, pp. 45 - 49, 67, 68)

Apart from integration, qualitative improvements are indispensable. Reliability, cost-efficiency and safety as well as efficiency and flexibility are the big plus factors of the road sector. An action package adopted by the EU in order has already been brought under way, targeting at simplified administration and strengthened competitiveness of European operators in this environment. (cp. EU-Mar 2006, p. 4)

A better infrastructure including quick, flexible and easy ways to transport larger quantities via water is essentially needed in view of growing demand for port capacities to handle the huge masses of containers arriving in Europe's ports. Also, the connection to the respective hinterlands is to be improved to handle the mentioned quantities efficiently. Accompanied should that be by a common maritime area allowing easier tracking and legal processing. (cp. EU-Mar 2006, p. 5, 6)

---

[15] Please see annex, figure 5.

Security is another key point to take care of. The famous averages of 'Erika' and 'Prestige' provide good, or rather bad, examples of maritime disasters in Union waters. Too few vessels currently sail under the EU flag, signifying a too bad compliance with the Union's security and safety standards including rigid regulations and regular checks (cp. Braun-Moser 1989, p. 47; cp. EU-Mar 2006, pp. 7 - 11)

Last, but not all least, the environmental concerns are to be included in the future actions as well. This is necessary since the energy efficiency and the pollution balance of vessels is not always as good as publicly assumed. Particularly ships under non-EU flags often do not respect the regulations. Stricter enforcement of the sanctions against violators thus will be an appropriate action to solve the problem. (cp. EU-Mar 2006, p. 12; EU-TPO 2006, pp. 16, 17)

3. The White Paper of the European Commission from 2001

Having gone through all the problems and challenges haunting Europe's transport sector, the 2001 White Paper 'European transport policy for 2010 – Time to decide' provides a set of concepts and approaches to get hold of the situation. The quintessence of the document is the necessity to concentrate on sustainable solutions of current problems in the Union's transport sector. The concepts presented by the Commission in the document should address the situational challenges in the entire transport sector exactly in that manner.

Since the bill is divided into four dimensions, each including a set of legislative recommendations and targets, this essay will assume the division to explain the concrete concepts. It should be bared in mind that a White Paper aims at setting the legal framework and the budgetary support by the European Union for a certain development. Operators and other players should then act accordingly.

1.   Shifting the modal balance

Bearing in mind the present modal split situation, two goals appeared are worth being pursued acc. to the Commission. A fiercer, albeit controlled, competition between the modes and a common strategy encouraging intermodality should help to accomplish the goal.

As regards the rivalry between the modes, an improvement of the road sector is one piece in the range of intended measures, among which the extension of the road network, i.e. building new international axes and some development in the new member states, takes a key role. A restructuring is necessary since the costs of road usage are artificially reduced, allowing the attractiveness of the sector to enhance. Corrective actions in this range are as much important as the enforcement of the Union's social norms and the promotion of SMEs in the industry and their mergers. In some areas, the creation of the legislative set-up has to be initiated at first though. In the coming years, infrastructural extension will no longer represent the majority of measures whereas the focus will be clearly laid on better capacity utilization and a better coordination with the neighbouring countries. (cp. EU-Road 2007, pp. 11, 12; cp. EU-WP 2001, pp. 23 – 27; cp. OECD7 2007)

In addition, the rail sector has to be 'revitalized', as the officials in Brussels would call it. Taking the bad state of European railways into account, a further integration of the mode into a common Internal Market is as inevitable as the optimisation of the use of existing capacities. To the former, especially the soaring volume of goods transportation needs an appropriate additional legal assistance (e.g. reg. cabotage, safety and security issues, interoperability and intermodality, yet also competitiveness). Stricter enforcement of present jurisdiction (e.g. providing improved conditions for cross-border transports and caring for more security for passenger and goods) would contribute to a better functioning of existing capacities, in the view of the Commission. Additionally, the current priority for passenger trains over goods trains has to be loosened to ensure higher reliability, speed and punctuality of the latter. Moreover, new and modern services are also needed urgently precisely because the perceived quality level is pretty low among (potential) customers. The intended high-speed tracks can play a good role to solve the problem, so can a concentration on services in the regional and local transit. (cp. ERRAC 2004, pp. 6, 10, 13, 16, 19, 22, 25, 28, 31, 36 - 39; cp. EU-WP 2001, pp. 27 - 36)

After road and rail, air traffic has also been eyed by the Commissioner and his employees. The recent dynamics in growth and acceptance as a usual transport mode has led to very well developed infrastructure with certain main hubs and many regional airports but, in the meantime, also to the comprehension that control schemes are necessary to avoid congestion levels like in the road sector. The congestion on ground and in the air should be remedied with the help of an intended common air traffic management system in the EU. Organisations like EuroControl[16] also have indicated their willingness to welcome the introduction of such a system,

---

[16] European Organisation for the Safety of Air Navigation, dealing with of issues of air traffic control.

not least with the purpose of indemnification of the world's highest air traffic safety and security standards. The strict enforcement of these standards and requirements is to be promoted, predominantly in the new enlargement member states. Helpful in this regard may the 'single sky'[17] initiative to complete the creation of an Internal Market. The definition of the legal scope, the obtaining of acceptance in the society via information and advertisement and the setting-out of the ranges of feasibility belong to the core tasks here. Apart from that, more support for the development of further hubs can help to upgrade efficiency of the air traffic in the entire Union. Never to be left out of sight are the environmental concerns, particularly regarding emissions and noise which are expected to aggravate in consequence of the growing traffic volume. (cp. EU-WP 2001, pp. 36 - 40; cp. Ewers/Tegner 2002, pp. 12 - 21)

Along with the competition between the modes, the cooperation should also be advanced, leading to intermodal solutions. Based on the modal split distribution, intermodality is viewed as a central tool to higher efficiency. Profiting from its good maritime infrastructure and the good waterway connection due to its major streams, the water-borne transport modes in Europe play a vital role here as they constitute an effective alternative well-worth considering. Despite the unequal distribution, the inland waterways have spare potential whose exploitation with the help of a support programme called 'Naiades' can alleviate the dramatic situation on Europe's roads. One condition and catalyst for further acceptance of this mode is a better endowed infrastructure, ranging from the establishment of so-called sea motorways to an increase in number and capacities of the commercial sea ports in the Union. Especially considering the upcoming infrastructural bottlenecks in consequence of the expected boost in container traffic at European sea ports, this appears highly crucial. So-called ea motorways should help to promote the acceptance of the mode in the way that fast and uncomplicated conveyance via water can be guaranteed. These motorway projects are to contribute to a network of "high-quality, integrated short-sea shipping connections" (from: EU-Mar 2006, p. 5), offering the flexibility demanded by customers. With the introduction of the sea motorways as a substitute to road routes and the promotion of short-sea shipping[18], the use of the maritime modes shall be encouraged. With that, a better capacity utilization of both ships and waterways is hoped to be achieved. Sustainable projects, like the wind-based vessel

---

[17] Sometimes also referred to as the "Single European Sky" initiative.
[18] This already happens between different ports, e.g. Hamburg-Göteborg and Rotterdam-Antwerpen.

drive system 'SkySails', are promoted as well. (cp. EU-Mar 2006, p. 5 - 11; cp. EU-WP 2001, pp. 41 - 46; cp. INE n.d.; cp. SkySails 2006)

By encouraging more vessels to sail under the EU flag, inter alia with financial benefits, and, thereby, to comply with Union's security and safety standards including rigid regulations and regular checks, the Commission tries parallelly to raise the security level at the European coasts, both regarding damage to persons and to nature. Likewise, security against any form of hazard, e.g. terrorist attacks or accidents like fires, is held vital. This refers to both the ports and the intermodal chains. An "effective accident response" is also highly valued, so is the impulse for new working and social conditions for the crews. Moreover, a common maritime area is considered to be able to be supportive in this endeavour as it allows easier tracking and legal processing. In this area, neighbouring countries and ones of strategic value[19] would be included. Also belonging to the topic of infrastructural expansion, a better hinterland connection of the sea ports is included in the considerations. Internal ports, rail tracks and highways from and to the sea ports make sure a smooth and efficient removal of the goods from quay and haulage to the correct destinations. (cp. Braun-Moser 1989, p. 47; cp. EU-Mar 2006, p. 5 - 11; cp. EU-WP 2001, pp. 41 - 46; cp. Van de Voorde/Viegas 1995, pp. 36 - 42)

The programme 'Marco Polo' is directed to the promotion of intermodal solutions and to the shift of traffic volume from the road to other modes by supporting companies acting in this way and making best-practices public throughout the Union. Also, investments to facilitate the changeovers belong to the objectives of the programme. Meanwhile, 'Marco Polo II' has come into stream, covering also environmental considerations. (cp. BMVBS3 2007, pp. 16, 17; cp. EU-Freight 2006, p. 5; cp. EU-WP 2001, pp. 46, 47)

In general, flexibility of the modes other than road is often considered to be very limited. Door-to-door transports are a real exception, so the road is still needed as a mode. But this does not apply to the entire distance whereby changeovers between the modes, and the required time, act their part of the decision. Consolidators are companies which compose an optimal combination of different transport modes for the respective sections of the route. The Commission intends to support such market operators. It also invests in R&D projects related to a smoother functioning of intermodality, e.g. in a research project about standardized containers for an easier

---

[19] For a common maritime sector, the EU has identified the following countries, among others, as strategically valuable partners: Russian Federation, South Korea, PR China and India.

transhipment from ships to trains. (cp. EU-ILU 2002, pp. 3 - 7; cp. EU-WP 2001, pp. 47, 48)

2.   Tackling bottlenecks

After times of parallel growth of both economy and traffic, signs of upcoming shortages in all modes are already visible at the horizon. Solving them successfully is a prerequisite for a completed Internal Market. The shortages, or bottlenecks, as the Commission prefers to name them, exist both on the side of the infrastructure and on the one of funding.

With reference to infrastructural bottlenecks, a four-dimensional relief package, esp. for the great axes through the Union territory, has been planned by Brussels.

Mainly, the package refers to the so-called 'trans-European network'. While the term, often abbreviated with TEN/-T, generally describes the totality of Union-wide networks of energy, telecommunication and transportation[20], it is used as a synonym for those projects related to transportation. The meanwhile 30 projects[21] are a response to different, partly long-standing, infrastructural deficits, ranging across all modes but with a strong focus on the rail network.[22] (cp. Himanen et al 1995, pp. 50 - 61; cp. EU-TEN1 2005; cp. EU-TEN2 2005, pp. 3 - 7)

Above all, multimodal corridors with a priority for freight haulage are to be established. When considering the thirty projects, some of them promote the construction of multimodal axes between various points of infrastructural interest like ports or main urban agglomerations. Especially for freight transports, the transportation on rail tracks and on water is to be pushed ahead, acc. to the Commissioner. In the light of ever increasing container traffic, this appears inescapable. Therefore, a good connection to other carriers is as elementary as the construction of special track lines for freight trains circumventing centres with high passenger volume. However, not only for freight, also for passenger carriage relief is a decisive term. Exemplarily, high-speed connections are pinned the hope of a whole mode on to reverse the tragic decay of the rail's role. Intermodal solutions, i.e. good rail connections to ferry ports and aerodromes, are equally aimed at. However, air traffic is wished to enhance much more due to the emissions released. (cp. EU-WP 2001, pp. 51 - 53; cp. EU-Freight 2007, pp. 6, 7)

---

[20]   TEN-T is an abbreviation for the transport-related projects of the Trans-European Network.
[21]   Initially, there existed the so-called 'Essen list' with fourteen projects.
[22]   Please see annex, figure 6.

Infrastructural relief also refers to the road network. Apart from sporadic extension of the latter, esp. in the eastern member states, the focus here lies with the optimal capacity utilization and traffic management, which both can take place by means of technological systems, infrastructural adjustments and legal realignments. (cp. EU-WP 2001, p. 53)

Moreover, the TEN-T projects want to deal with certain problem areas, e.g. the mountain ranges of the Alps and the Pyrenees, where restricted permeability and congestion, on the one hand, and safety concerns particularly in tunnels, on the other, claim immediate act. (cp. EU-WP 2001, pp. 53 - 58) Some of the residual projects like Galileo, Europe's satellite-based radio navigation programme, will be introduced in a later chapter.

Funding from the public authorities is always a meagre business but for transport infrastructure projects raising private funds has proven to be similarly burdensome. Innovative financing schemes therefore become increasingly interesting for the stakeholders of such projects.

Hitherto, cross-border projects, often for freight transports, did not enjoy the attention and preferential treatment like the ones of purely national and passenger-related interests, which still prioritised roads. Such practices are no longer to be supported by the Union, much less in these times of empty coffers. Specialisation in sustainable projects of strategic importance to the Community will be preferred, acc. to the Commissioner. (cp. EU-WP 2001, pp. 58, 59) With its funding the EU can manage the development towards its very own visions, i.e. with preference for those undertakings including interoperability of different systems or better connectivity of remote areas. In contrast to former restrictions to a maximum EU contribution of 10%, new alignment would punctually allow higher grants.

Higher significance as a source enjoy private investors. (cp. EU-WP 2001, p. 59) As a consequence of previous projects, low profitability and high financial insecurity are associated, resulting from the huge initial expenditures, the long waiting times until the first receipts and the slow amortisation. In default of broader acceptance, public-private partnerships have not established as effective solutions yet, despite EU authorities promising to assume the risks.

Innovative funding is therefore a preferred option for the EU presently. To these belong the spending of tax revenues and the practice of cross-financing, i.e. the charging of infrastructure use in a region in which a new construction is projected. (cp. EU-WP 2001, pp. 60 - 62) This may imply the targeted charging of tolls for the use of one or more specific alternative routes or of all routes in the surrounding region. For that method, some legal amendments are still to be finalized though.

3.   Putting users first

After having discussed various topics within European transport policy, pertaining to different players in the sector, the users have not been explicitly considered. Just as in this essay, the European Commission neither wants to disregard this central group of participants in the industry and its main demands and needs. To these belong the aspects of traffic safety, costing and taxation, accessibility and affordability as well as urban mobility management.

Regarding what "the people of Europe [call their] prime concern" (from: EU-WP 2001, p. 65) the European Commission aims for a noticeable decrease of the far too high number of road fatalities. (cp. EU-WP 2001, pp. 65 – 70; cp. EuroStat10 n.d.) Realizing the existing jurisdiction more severely is as much part of the plan as implementing (and using) new, common and more effective penalty programmes and technological aids. (cp. BMVBS3 2007, pp. 39 - 41) The projected measures, ranging from new driving license and training standards as well as stricter working and social norms for lorry drivers as far as universal traffic signs and new safety regulations for both vehicle and infrastructure operators, has already been accepted among the large number of stakeholders. Telematics and other intelligent systems for traffic management and anti-collision should also help to contribute.

Another point to be mentioned is the financial impact of infrastructure construction and provision in the European Union. From the Commission's point of view, time has come that Europeans should learn the reality behind the falsified cost calculation of the precious commodity called mobility. The authorities in Brussels compass the installation of incentives for the use of sustainable modes and policies of deterrence for artificially cheapened modes. (cp. EU-WP 2001, pp. 71 - 77) Also, a more just charging of tolls corresponding to the real use of the property with the individual vehicle is aspired, possibly including emerging social (e.g. fatalities) and external (e.g. emissions, noise, climate change) costs. This would probably rather apply to goods carriers than to passenger transporters due to their higher quantity and intensity of use. The earned money then is destined for the promotion of more sustainable and eco-friendly modes. Not only because of this is an EU-wide integrated management of all modes badly needed. So as to let it become reality though, the suitable legal framework has to be set up. Charging tolls is a difficult game as the balance between costs and taxes has to be preserved since otherwise a uniform and cause-fair practice is practically impossible. The harmonization of the fuel taxation across the EU takes the same line. Current competitive disadvantages are to be eliminated with corresponding assimilation steps. At the same time, tax incentives for alternative fuels like bio-fuels can help to advance in the pursuit of sustainability in the sector. (cp. EU-WP 2001, pp. 71 – 77; cp. EurActiv 2007)

Not only should the transport sector enable further exploitation according to the rules of market economy, but it should also serve its role as a basic commodity for the citizens in the Union. (cp. EU-WP 2001, pp. 79 - 81) Therefore, sustainability in terms of intermodal solutions and eco-friendly modes is of public interest. As to the user, this impacts his everyday life (and lifestyle) while he or she has to become more aware of his or her rights and duties as a responsible member of the society. Intermodality in passenger traffic is connected with a bunch of complicated processes, esp. during the changeovers from one mode to another. If a German person from Bremen, for instance, plans to take a holiday in Faro, Portugal, he might have to take the bus to come to the central station, where he catches his train to the airport. After the flight to Faro, he might have to take a cab to the hotel. For each and every of the different modes, he needs separate tickets and, beyond it, in many occasions he has to take care of his luggage on his own. Ticketing and luggage handling services will have to be improved to promote the idea of intermodality in passenger traffic which delivers the reason for the Commission to address the difficulty. Services for earlier registration of luggage and for universal tickets are thus to be supported, as much as constructional adjustments. (cp. EU-WP 2001, pp. 77 - 79) As mentioned before, educating the users about their rights and duties and inducing reconsideration of lifestyle and behaviour belongs to the intended goals of the Commission. Mannerful behaviour, esp. for safety reasons, is common practice aboard of aircrafts and trains. So should be the compensation or refunding for losses, accidents, and delays, yet also the appreciation of complaints. Promoting good examples and creating awareness is the primary goal here.

Assistance with the rationalization of urban transport and with its simultaneous presentation to the customer is another user-related task the EU has assigned to itself. Rationalisation is sought by diversification of the energy sources used, i.e. the promotion of alternative fuels, and, again, by promoting best-practices already in use. (cp. EU-WP 2001, pp. 81 - 85; cp. EurActiv 2007; cp. GIC 2007, pp. 41 - 52)

4.   The global dimension of European transport

The global dimension refers to both the enlargement rounds of 2004 and 2007 and the international bodies in which the EU has had an observer role only.

After the decades of the Iron Curtain, both infrastructural modernisation and harmonisation and the related fund-raising efforts are the main issues of eastern enlargement in this field. The infrastructural links between Western and Eastern Europe have to be built urgently as soaring goods transport volumes lead to swift congestion of the few east-west axes. The historically good position of eastern railway can merely be used constrictedly as the network is outdated and, thus, probably inappropriate for today's needs like just-in-time. (cp. EU-WP 2001, pp. 89 - 92) Regarding the maritime modes, the safety aspect has to be highlighted by a better organisation of shipping, more supervision as well as stricter rules on technology, social norms, flags of convenience and illegal immigration. With the new states, the number of potential participants in a common sea traffic management system and the respective coordination demand rises.

Moreover, the European Union needs an own voice in international organisations, a single European voice. (cp. EU-WP 2001, pp. 92, 93) On merely being represented by the member states, which were not obliged to the EU guidelines, the capacity to act is rather restricted. Especially in multinational bodies coordinating the traffic on main transport axes, such as major rivers, this becomes apparent.

Regarding air traffic, the new vista of European politicians has wandered to the implementation of the EU approach to neighbouring countries and to key strategic partners[23], after having created a quite comfortable home position on Union territory. (cp. EU-Air 2007, pp. 5 – 11) In the past, bilateral agreements with the respective nations were used. These agreements were confined to the use of those national carriers whose nations were concerned by the flight. According to Union law though, such a passage is unlawful. The regulations in the partner countries oftentimes were equally complicated, as the example of the United States clearly shows. (cp. EU-WP 2001, pp. 93, 94) After partly long negotiations and some complicated reorganisation works the present bilateral agreements have integrated Union clauses so that their

---

[23]   For the air transport sector, the EU has identified the following countries as key partners: United States, Canada, Australia, New Zealand, Chile, PR China and India.

conformity with the legal prerequisites is safeguarded. Thereby, the so-called 'open skies' agreement is to be enforced, saying that any European carrier can depart from any European airport to any destination of the partner country. With this, the benefits of a common Internal Market are to be transferred to the neighbours and strategic partners. Not altruism, but solid economic and social benefits for the Union constitute the motivation behind this approach.

Last but not at all least, the civil satellite-based radio navigation programme of the EU, Galileo will be presented. (cp. EU-WP 2001, pp. 94, 95) It is said to be the world's most sophisticated navigation programme, allowing applications not solely from the transport sector but from many industries. The Commission wishes to avoid being "totally dependent on third countries in such a strategic area" (from: EU-WP 2001, p. 95), as the competitive services[24] are chiefly designed for military use and thus less reliable for Europe. (cp. EU-Galileo 2005, pp. 5, 7 – 11, 15 – 19, 29 – 31) Concerning the sector, new traffic management systems may base upon the technology offered by Galileo. However, the implementation runs rather sluggishly.

4. Barriers to a quicker development

In spite of all ambitious aspirations, the progress is caught in a crossfire of impeding influences from different angles.

Above all, financial shortages hinder the quick and thorough adoption of the Commission's recommendations. As explained earlier, finding private money sources has become troublesome as raising public funds.

Geographical reasons are also opposed to such a development. (cp. Button 1992, p. 34) These include both natural factors like tunnels through compact mountain ranges or over waters, yet also political motives such as the Union's external borders, where the operational sphere of Brussels ends. In both cases, infrastructural extension requires intensified coordination of efforts. One example is the 'open skies' agreements with the United States.

The state of the infrastructure itself can also act as an obstacle to further acceptance of a corresponding mode since issues like lacking interoperability, obsolete properties, quality deficits and too high assimilation requirements get in the way of it. (cp. Button 1992, p. 36)

Thereby, economic attractiveness is also reduced since lower profitability and slower amortisation are said to come along with such projects. This particularly applies to

---

[24] Competitors of Galileo are the military services 'GPS' (United States) and 'Glonass' (Russia).

certain 'out-of-fashion' modes like rail tracks and to the provision of latest intermodal solutions.

Tardiness in the legal environment is also a fact the processes are facing, as could and still can be seen at the reform process of critical regulations like the 'open skies' settlement and the permission of cabotage. The institutional conditions still favour this insufficiency since effective implementation measures are missing. (cp. Button 1992, pp. 36, 37)

National governments are a decisive level since they have to reduce EU directives and recommendations to practice by putting them into national legislation. In former times, national movements like strong pressure groups of traditionally influential industries and suspicious citizens urged the governments to adopt protectionist (and other counterproductive) measures and, hence, to disregard the benefits of an Internal Market.

Worsening problems like noise, emissions and fatalities are aspects that the Commission is no longer willing to accept. So, environmental and social aspects have to play a role in considerations regarding future projects. This was resolved in 2001 in the context of the adoption of a common sustainability strategy. Thereby, some promising projects might fail due to insufficient compliance with the strict EU guidelines. (EC-Got 2001, pp. 5 - 9)

Acceptance in the society can be two-edged sword since sometimes long-term beneficial aspirations are rejected due to small-minded and short-sighted reasons. Especially cost increases are such a reason which means that the moderation of the real infrastructure costs, envisaged by the Commission in its White Paper, might become delicate challenge. Likewise, people sometimes do not forgive the quality shortcomings, in the starting phase after a initiation in particular, which again can impede the establishment of that project.

IV. The obtained so far and the obtainables in future

By having referred to the 2006 Mid-term review during the presentation of current situation in the European transport sector, most interim results have already been presented earlier. Generally, it becomes obvious that progresses are made only sluggishly. In addition, the modal split balance is expected to remain stable. So, apart from certain exceptions, many premises do not change for the following action fields.

The tardiness of the national governments might have to do with the amount of work connected with a transposition of the Commission's recommendations, yet also with more urgent problems prevailing. Be that as it may, all that did not prevent the Commissioner and his subordinates to place new impulses in various fields again and again.

In the road sector, the modal shift is given top priority, esp. in the face of the huge pressure awaited due to forecasted rise in container traffic. Likewise, the idea of charging tolls for infrastructure use is currently being discussed and will probably even be strengthened in future. Internalising external cost and, thereby, conveying the truth to the citizens is another goal for the nearer future, in particular in the times of aggravated climate change. Naturally, the realisation of the road projects, e.g. of the TEN-T list, belongs to the key tasks, too.

The latter is also applicable to the rail sector with its multiplicity of TEN-T projects arranged. So far, the number of partly or fully completed connections is rather low, so both pressure and assistance might be necessary to ignite the undertakings. Negotiations on interoperability will constitute another task among the ones of the rail mode, just as the better prioritisation of freight transports on railways.

Apart from a further boost of the 'Naiades' programme for inland waterways and of a common sea port policy, the set-up of a common maritime traffic area appears on the agenda, too. Such a common area is also aimed for in the air sector, along with a suitable common air traffic management system. Besides, the bilateral agreements with neighbour countries and strategic partners should be finalized as well as the focus laid on airport capacity amplification and optimised utilisation.

Moreover, further aspects of realisation of decided TEN-T projects, funding and legal frameworks will call the Commission's attention many times. Galileo is estimated to be able to go on line by 2013 in case of smooth preparations. The promotion of intermodal solutions under sustainability standpoints will also take a role of major interest of the Commission, mainly with the help of its programme 'Marco Polo II'. Concrete decisions in this regard can be expected in the coming years.

The undisputedly dominating issue, however, is the environmental concern, be it hiddenly included or openly disclosed as a goal. Promoting projects leading to efficiency increases, safety enhancement and social benefits thus belongs to the key tasks.

V. Conclusion

After having considered the different sections of the transport policy in Europe, one can draw several conclusions. Sustained economic growth, which will continue to belong to the top priorities of the European Union, should be uncoupled from the rise in traffic volume. Therefore, efficiency and utilization rates have to be improved. At the same time though, environmental and social consequences of further growth has to be scanned carefully.

The present modal split situation has revealed an advanced dominance of the road over other modes in both passenger and goods transport segments. However, difficulties currently rule the picture of the mode. Growth in the air traffic leads to similar problems, yet again to higher mobility of the citizens. Infrastructural extension is of secondary interest for these two modes, efficiency and safety issues are focused upon.

Emanating from this, spare capacities of other modes must be used to relieve the road sector and to optimise goods and passenger flow across Union territory. It is up to the following two modes to accomplish the goal of a modal shift. The main 'problem child' still is the railway sector with decreasing investments and devastated acceptance, mainly due to too few prearrangements to facilitate cross-border, transports competitively. Similarly, the rather unfavourable situation of the maritime transport sector is to be eliminated as well. Selective measures, such as a number of projects within the TEN-T project arrangement, should help to provide an infrastructure capable of dealing with the expected huge demands.

Modal shift will not only take place by complete shifts away from the road sector since it offers a high reliability and flexibility at low prices. Yet, the processing of some route sections with modes other than the road may already contribute to a noticeable relief for Europe. So, it is dedicated strategies for the respective modes as well as a strong promotion of long-sighted and sustainable intermodal solutions should help to realize the modal shift.

Having said that, a modal shift can only take place properly only when shortages in other modes are tackled. In this regard, fund-raising is highly estimated as well. With scarce funds, the focus on really sustainable projects is expected to turn out even more clearly.

The farsighted concentration on the needs of the users shall neither be dropped from the agenda. Safety issues and an allocation of the true costs top the list here while convenience aspects and rationalisation, including environmental and social topics, also might affect users. Taking a more and more globalised world into consideration, Europe needs an own voice to strengthen its own influence in the world. This refers to the membership in political and economic bodies, yet also in active contributions, e.g. new technologies like Galileo.

Above all stands the idea of implementing the core theme of sustainability into the transport sector. A wise coordination of economic and political motivation belongs to a long-term provision of functioning and effective transports sector as much as a stronger regard of environmental and social concerns.

Annex

Figure 1: Modal split of freight transport and passenger transport in the EU-25

(2005 figures, based on tonne-kilometres performed)   (2004 figures, based on passenger-kilometres performed)

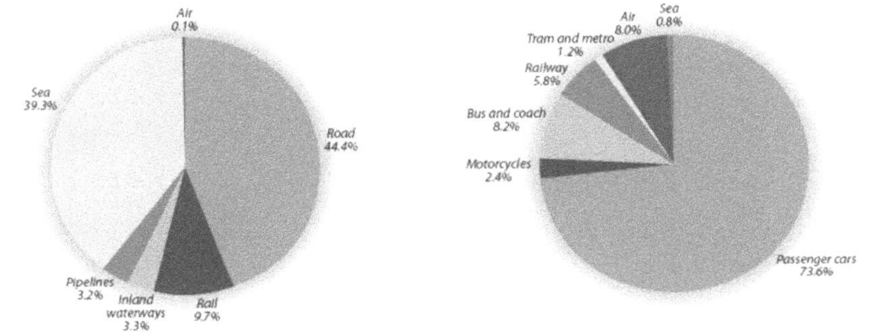

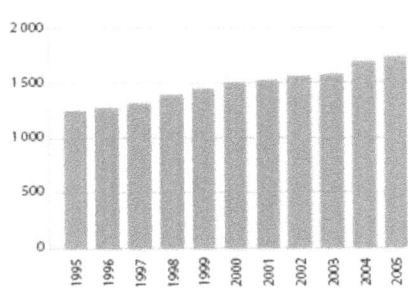

Source[25]: European Commission, 2007

Figure 2: Growth in road transport in the EU-25
(billion tonne-kilometres)

Source[26]: European Commission, 2006

[25] This figure can be found at: EU-Road 2007, p. 2
[26] This figure can be found at: EU-Road 2007, p. 3

Figure 3: Number of flight routes (from city to city in the EU-27)

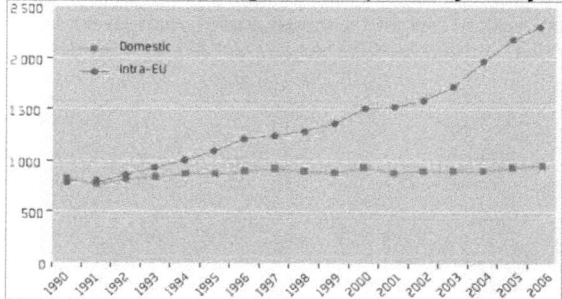

Source[27]: European Commission, 2007

---

[27]   This figure can be found at: EU-Air 2007, p. 5

Figure 4: Different electrical power supplies used in Europe

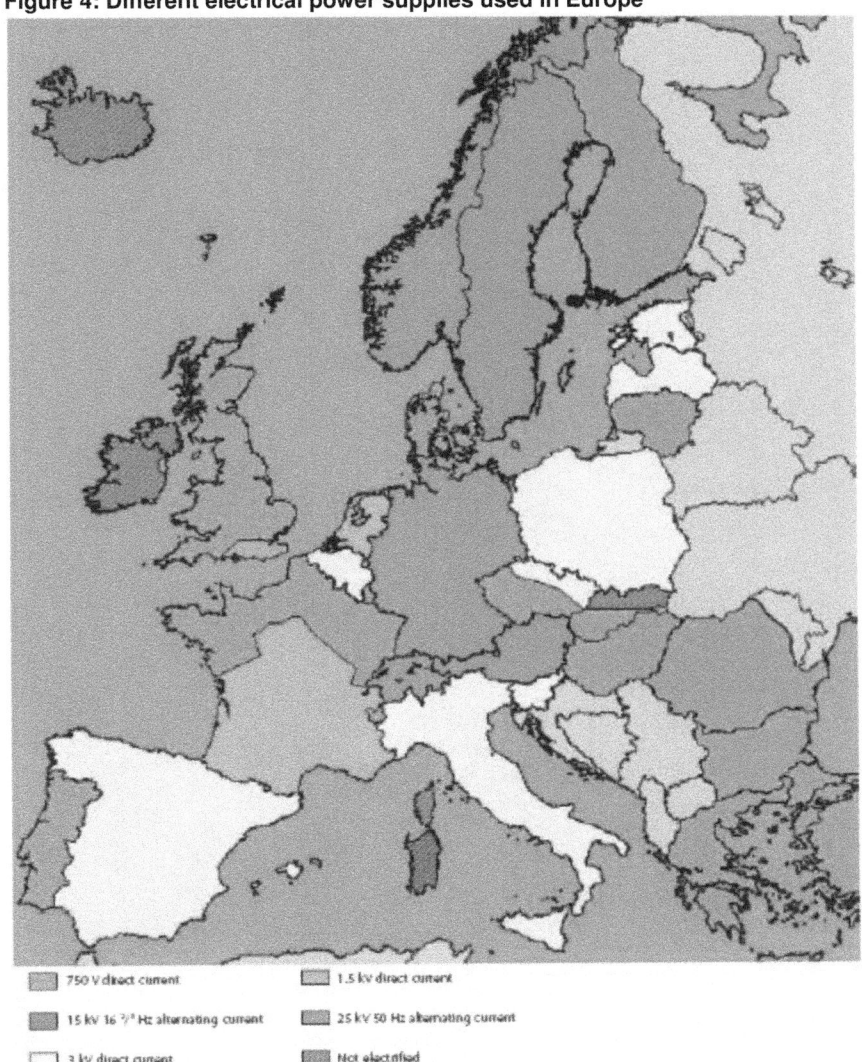

▨	750 V direct current	▨	1.5 kV direct current
▨	15 kV 16 ⅔ Hz alternating current	▨	25 kV 50 Hz alternating current
☐	3 kV direct current	▨	Not electrified

Source[28]: European Commission, 2003

---

[28] This figure can be found at: EU-Rail 2003, p. 5

Figure 5: Europe's main industrial ports

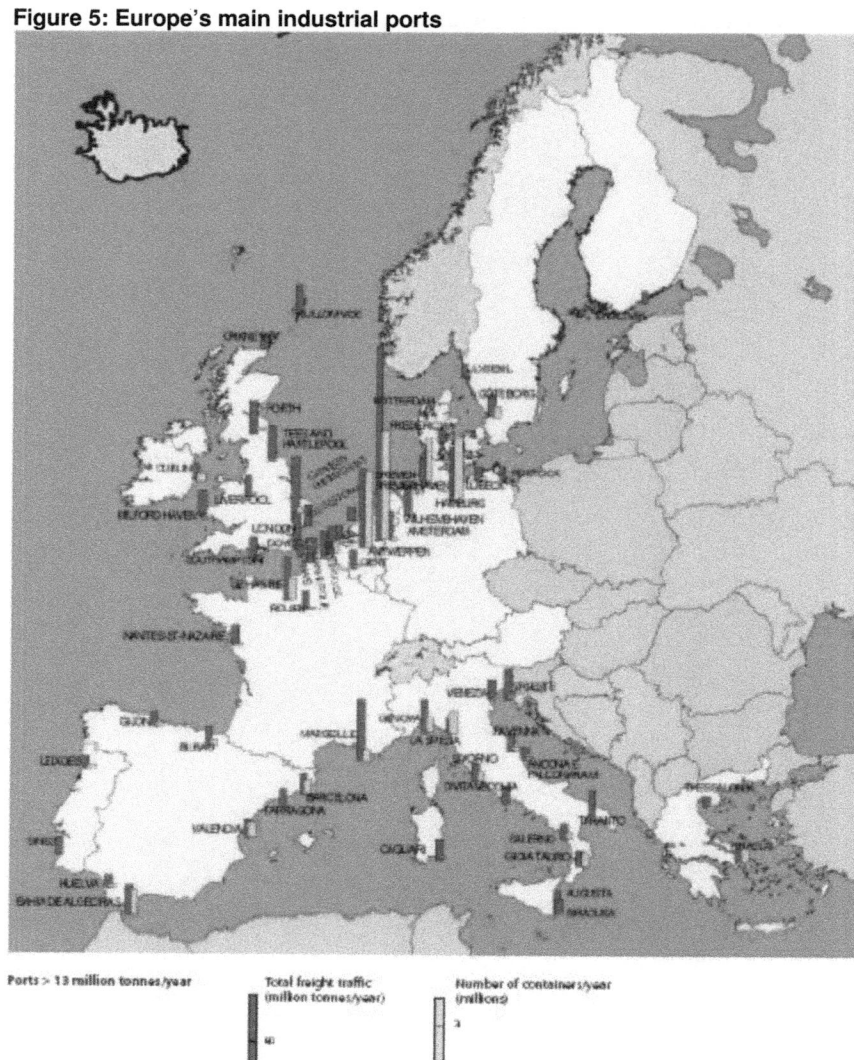

Source[29]: European Commission, 2001

---

[29] This figure can be found at: EU-WP 2001, p. 43

Figure 6: Trans-European Network projects

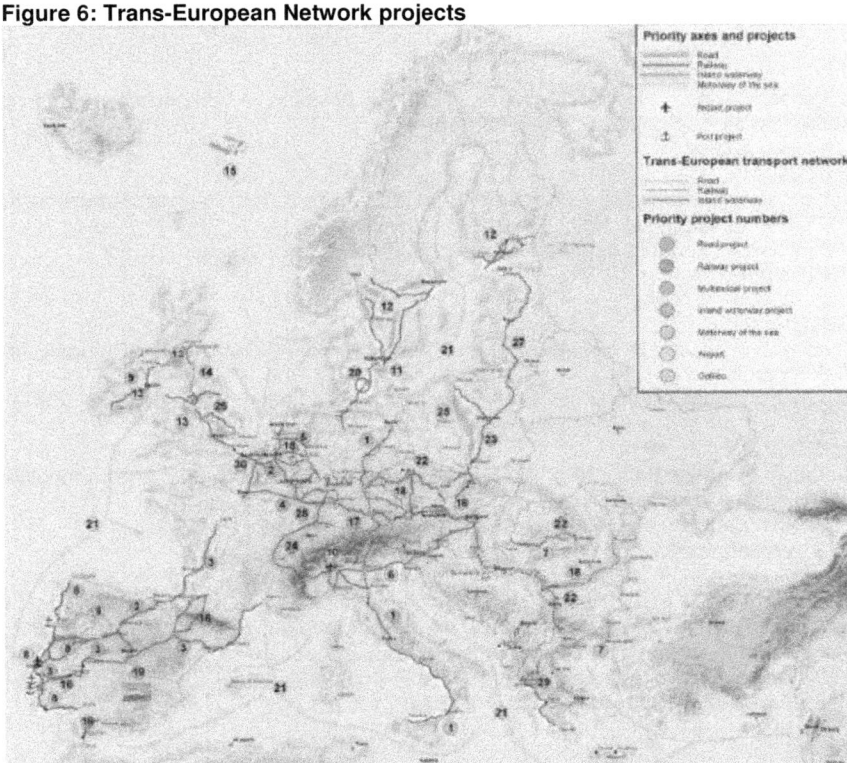

Source[30]: European Commission, 2006

---

[30]   This figure can be found at: EU-TEN 2006, pp. 12, 13

Bibliography

Ammoser/Hoppe 2006
Ammoser, H./ Hoppe, M. (2006): Glossar Verkehrswesen und Verkehrswissenschaften. Dresden (Germany).

BBR 2005
Bundesamt für Bauwesen und Raumordnung (ed.) (2001): Raumordnungsbericht 2005. Kernaussagen und wichtige Abbildungen.
http://www.starkenburg.de/uploads/media/ROB2005_Kernaussagen_01.pdf (13.12.2007)

BMVBS1 2007
Bundesministerium für Verkehr, Bau und Stadtentwicklung (ed.) (2007): Europäische Verkehrspolitik.
http://www.bmvbs.de/Verkehr/-,1424/Europaeische-Verkehrspolitik.htm (11.11.2007)

BMVBS2 2007
Bundesministerium für Verkehr, Bau und Stadtentwicklung (ed.) (2007): Europapolitik im BMVBS – Verkehrspolitik.
http://www.bmvbs.de/EU-Ratspraesidentschaft/Europapolitik-im-BMVBS-,2723/Verkehrspolitik.htm (12.11.2007)

BMVBS3 2007
Bundesministerium für Verkehr, Bau und Stadtentwicklung (ed.) (2007): Kompendium der EU-Verkehrspolitik. Ausgabe August 2007.
http://www.bmvbs.de/Anlage/original_1018078/Kompendium-der-EU-Verkehrspolitik-Stand-August-2007-barrierefrei.pdf (13.12.2007)

BMWi 2007
Bundesministerium für Wirtschaft und Technologie (ed.) (2007): Mobilität und Verkehr. Nachhaltigkeit, Sicherheit und Wettbewerbsfähigkeit durch intelligenten Verkehr.
http://www.bmwi.de/BMWi/Redaktion/PDF/mobilitaet-und-verkehr,property=pdf,bereich=bmwi,sprache=de,rwb=true.pdf (13.12.2007)

BPB 2005
Bundeszentrale für politische Bildung (Hrsg.) (2005): Europäische Union. (Informationen zur politischen Bildung, Heft 279). Revised volume. Bonn (Germany).

Braun-Moser 1989
Braun-Moser, Ursula (1989): Europäische Verkehrspolitik – Chancen und Ziele. Sindelfingen (Germany).

Brundtland 1987
UN World Commission on Environment and Development (ed.) (1987): Our Common Future. Report of the World Commission on Environment and Development. Oxford (UK).

Button 1992
Button, K. (ed.) (1992): Das integrierte europäische Verkehrskonzept.

In: Button, Kenneth (ed.): Europäische Verkehrspolitik – Wege in die Zukunft. Strategien und Optionen für die Zukunft Europas. Gütersloh (Germany). P. 26 - 81.

DIB 2000
Deutscher IngenieurInnen Bund e.V. (ed.) (2000): Nachhaltiger Verkehr – kann es das geben?. (dib Rundbrief Nr. 55, 4/00: Nachhaltigkeit). Darmstadt (Germany).
http://www.dibev.de/fakten/rba_pdf/verkehr.pdf (13.12.2007)

EC-Got 2001
European Commission (ed.) (2001): Communication from the Commission: A Sustainable Europe for a Better World: A European Union Strategy for Sustainable Development.
http://europa.eu/eur-lex/en/com/cnc/2001/com2001_0264en01.pdf (01.01.2008)

ECB 2007
European Central Bank (ed.) (2007): Treaty establishing the European Community.
http://www.ecb.int/ecb/legal/pdf/maastricht_de.pdf (12.12.2007)

ECET1 2006
European Commission, Directorate-General for Energy and Transport (ed.) (2006): Energy & transport in figures 2006. Part 1: General data.
http://ec.europa.eu/dgs/energy_transport/figures/pocketbook/doc/2006/2006_general_en.pdf (08.11.2007)

ECET2 2006
European Commission, Directorate-General for Energy and Transport (ed.) (2006): Energy & transport in figures 2006. Part 2: Energy.
http://ec.europa.eu/dgs/energy_transport/figures/pocketbook/doc/2006/2006_energy_en.pdf (08.11.2007)

ECET3 2006
European Commission, Directorate-General for Energy and Transport (ed.) (2006): Energy & transport in figures 2006. Part 3: Transport.
http://ec.europa.eu/dgs/energy_transport/figures/pocketbook/doc/2006/2006_transport_en.pdf (08.11.2007)

ECET1 2007
European Commission, Directorate-General for Energy and Transport (ed.) (2007): Energy & transport in figures 2007. Part 2: Energy.
http://ec.europa.eu/dgs/energy_transport/figures/pocketbook/doc/2007/2007_energy_en.pdf (13.12.2007)

ECET2 2007
European Commission, Directorate-General for Energy and Transport (ed.) (2007): Building bridges. Extension of the major trans-European transport axes to the neighbouring countries.
http://ec.europa.eu/ten/transport/external_dimension/doc/2007_building_bridges_en.pdf (26.12.2007)

ECMT 2005
European Conference of Ministers of Transport (ed.) (2005): Trends in the Transport Sector. 1970 – 2003 (4th volume). Paris (France).

ECMT 2006
European Conference of Ministers of Transport (ed.) (2006): Inland waterways and
environmental protection. Summary (For official use). Paris (France).
http://www.cemt.org/online/council/2006/CM200610Fe.pdf (11.11.2007)

ECMT 2007
European Conference of Ministers of Transport (ed.) (2007): Railway accounts for
effective regulation. http://www.cemt.org/pub/pubpdf/07RailAcc.pdf (11.11.2007)

EC-Rail 2007
European Commission, Directorate-General for Energy and Transport (ed.) (2007):
Marktöffnung und –integration im Eisenbahnsektor der EU. Wien (Austria).
http://ec.europa.eu/transport/rail/overview/doc/js-wien-feb2007.pdf (11.11.2007)

ERRAC 2004
European Rail Research Advisory Council (ed.) (2004): Rail Research in the EU. A
comparison of Member State public research programmes with the ERRAC SRRA
2020. Brussels (Belgium). http://www.errac.org/docs/RailResearchinMS-042004.pdf
(01.01.2008)

EU-Air 2007
European Union (ed.) (2007): Flying together. EU Air Transport Policy.
http://ec.europa.eu/transport/air_portal/international/doc/brochures/2007_air_transpor
t_flying_together_en.pdf (12.11.2007)

EU-Freight 2006
European Commission, Directorate-General for Energy and Transport (ed.) (2006):
European freight transport. Modern logistics solutions for competitiveness and
sustainability.
http://ec.europa.eu/transport/logistics/documentation/highlights/doc/2006_brochure_f
reight_en.pdf (26.12.2007)

EU-Freight 2007
European Commission, Directorate-General for Energy and Transport (ed.) (2007):
Communication from the Commission. Freight Transport Logistics Action Plan.
http://ec.europa.eu/transport/logistics/freight_logistics_action_plan/doc/action_plan/2
007_com_logistics_action_plan_en.pdf (01.01.2008)

EU-Galileo 2005
European Space Agency (ed.) (2005): Galileo. The European Programme for Global
Navigation Services. Noordwijk (The Netherlands).
http://ec.europa.eu/dgs/energy_transport/galileo/documents/doc/2005_02_23_galileo
_en.pdf (01.01.2008)

EU-Got 2001
European Union (ed.) (2001): Presidency Conclusions. Göteborg European Council,
15 and 16 June 2001.
http://ec.europa.eu/governance/impact/docs/key_docs/goteborg_concl_en.pdf
(11.11.2007)

EU-Hist1 n.d.
European Union (ed.) (no date): 1990 – 1999. Ein Europa ohne Grenzen.
http://europa.eu/abc/history/1990-1999/index_de.htm (26.12.2007)

EU-Hist2 n.d.
European Union (ed.) (no date): 1992. Europäisches Jahr für Sicherheit, Hygiene und Gesundheit am Arbeitsplatz.
http://europa.eu/abc/history/1990-1999/1992/index_de.htm (26.12.2007)

EU-Hist3 n.d.
European Union (ed.) (no date): 1993. Europäisches Jahr der älteren Menschen und der Solidargemeinschaft der Generationen.
http://europa.eu/abc/history/1990-1999/1993/index_de.htm (26.12.2007)

EU-Hist4 n.d.
European Union (ed.) (no date): 1994. Europäisches Jahr der Ernährung.
http://europa.eu/abc/history/1990-1999/1994/index_de.htm (26.12.2007)

EU-Hist5 n.d.
European Union (ed.) (no date): 1997. Europäisches Jahr gegen Rassismus und Fremdenfeindlichkeit.
http://europa.eu/abc/history/1990-1999/1997/index_de.htm (26.12.2007)

EU-Hist6 n.d.
European Union (ed.) (no date): 1998.
http://europa.eu/abc/history/1990-1999/1998/index_de.htm (26.12.2007)

EU-Hist7 n.d.
European Union (ed.) (no date): 1999.
http://europa.eu/abc/history/1990-1999/1999/index_de.htm (26.12.2007)

EU-ILU 2002
European Commission, Directorate-General for Energy and Transport (ed.) (2002): Intermodal Loading Units. Harmonisation and Standardisation Initiative. Brussels (Belgium).
http://ec.europa.eu/transport/intermodality/legislation/doc/consultation-paper_en.pdf (01.01.08)

EU-Mar 2006
European Union (ed.) (2006): Maritime Transport Policy. Improving the competitiveness, safety and security of European shipping.
http://ec.europa.eu/transport/maritime/doc/maritime_transport_policy_en.pdf (12.11.2007)

EU-Rail 2003
European Union (ed.) (2003): Revitalising Europe's railways. Towards an integrated European railway area.
http://ec.europa.eu/transport/rail/overview/doc/brochure_en.pdf (26.12.2007)

EU-Rail 2007
European Union (ed.) (2007): Rail Transport and Interoperability. Rail transport: the current situation and the Commission's initiatives.

http://ec.europa.eu/transport/rail/overview/current_en.htm (26.12.2007)

EU-Road 2007
European Union (ed.) (2007): Road Transport Policy. Open Roads across Europe.
http://ec.europa.eu/transport/road/doc/road_transport_policy_en.pdf (12.11.2007)

EU-TEN1 2005
Europäische Union (ed.) (2005): Gemeinschaftliche Leitlinien für den Aufbau eines transeuropäischen Verkehrsnetzes. http://europa.eu/scadplus/leg/de/lvb/l24094.htm (12.11.2007)

EU-TEN2 2005
European Union (ed.) (2005): Trans-European Network. TEN-T priority axes and projects 2005. http://ec.europa.eu/ten/transport/projects/doc/2005_ten_t_en.pdf (14.11.2007)

EU-TPO 2006
European Union (ed.) (2006): Keep Europe Moving. Sustainable mobility for our continent.
http://ec.europa.eu/transport/transport_policy_review/doc/2006_3167_brochure_en.p df (30.10.2007)

EU-WP 2001
European Union (ed.) (2001): White Paper. European transport policy for 2010: time to decide. http://ec.europa.eu/transport/white_paper/index_en.htm (30.10.2007)

Eur-Lex (n.d.)
Eur-Lex (ed.) (no date): Treaty on European Union (1992). http://eur-lex.europa.eu/en/treaties/dat/11992M/htm/11992M.html (12.12.2007))

EurActiv 2004
EurActiv.com (ed.) (2004): Weißbuch Verkehrspolitik.
http://www.euractiv.com/de/verkehr/weibuch-verkehrspolitik/article-130033 (12.12.2007)

EurActiv1 2006
EurActiv.com (ed.) (2006): Verkehrspolitik - In Kürze.
http://www.euractiv.com/de/verkehr/verkehrspolitik-kurze/article-159395 (12.12.2007)

EurActiv2 2006
EurActiv.com (ed.) (2006): TEN-V: Aufbau eines transeuropäischen Verkehrsnetzes.
http://www.euractiv.com/de/verkehr/ten-v-aufbau-transeuropaischen-verkehrsnetzes/article-157380 (12.12.2007)

EurActiv 2007
EurActiv.com (ed.) (2007): Alternative fuels for transport.
http://www.euractiv.com/en/environment/alternative-fuels-transport/article-138101 (01.01.2008)

Eurordis 2007
Eurordis (ed.) (2007): The legislative acts: Regulations, Directives and other legislation. http://www.eurordis.org/article.php3?id_article=1557 (13.12.2007)

EuroStat1 n.d.
EuroStat (ed.) (no date): Gesamtenergieverbrauch des Verkehrs.
http://epp.eurostat.ec.europa.eu/pls/portal/url/page/PGP_QUEEN/PGE_QUEEN_DE
TAIL?screen=detailref&language=de&product=sdi_tr&root=sdi_tr/sdi_tr/sdi_tr1000
(08.11.2007)

EuroStat2 n.d.
EuroStat (ed.) (no date): Anteil des Straßentransports am gesamten inländischen
Güterverkehr.
http://epp.eurostat.ec.europa.eu/pls/portal/url/page/PGP_QUEEN/PGE_QUEEN_DE
TAIL?screen=detailref&language=de&product=sdi_tr&root=sdi_tr/sdi_tr/sdi_tr_gro/sdi
_tr1100 (08.11.2007)

EuroStat3 n.d.
EuroStat (ed.) (no date): Personenbeförderung nach Verkehrszweig.
http://epp.eurostat.ec.europa.eu/pls/portal/url/page/PGP_QUEEN/PGE_QUEEN_DE
TAIL?screen=detailref&language=de&product=sdi_tr&root=sdi_tr/sdi_tr/sdi_tr_gro/sdi
_tr1110 (08.11.2007)

EuroStat4 n.d.
EuroStat (ed.) (no date): Anteil des Straßentransports am gesamten inländischen
Güterverkehr.
http://epp.eurostat.ec.europa.eu/pls/portal/url/page/PGP_QUEEN/PGE_QUEEN_DE
TAIL?screen=detailref&language=de&product=sdi_tr&root=sdi_tr/sdi_tr/sdi_tr_gro/sdi
_tr1200 (08.11.2007)

EuroStat5 n.d.
EuroStat (ed.) (no date): Güterverkehr nach Verkehrszweig.
http://epp.eurostat.ec.europa.eu/pls/portal/url/page/PGP_QUEEN/PGE_QUEEN_DE
TAIL?screen=detailref&language=de&product=sdi_tr&root=sdi_tr/sdi_tr/sdi_tr_gro/sdi
_tr1210 (08.11.2007)

EuroStat6 n.d.
EuroStat (ed.) (no date): Güterverkehrsvolumen.
http://epp.eurostat.ec.europa.eu/pls/portal/url/page/PGP_QUEEN/PGE_QUEEN_DE
TAIL?screen=detailref&language=de&product=sdi_tr&root=sdi_tr/sdi_tr/sdi_tr_gro/sdi
_tr1220 (08.11.2007)

EuroStat7 n.d.
EuroStat (ed.) (no date): Energieverbrauch, nach Verkehrszweig.
http://epp.eurostat.ec.europa.eu/pls/portal/url/page/PGP_QUEEN/PGE_QUEEN_DE
TAIL?screen=detailref&language=de&product=sdi_tr&root=sdi_tr/sdi_tr/sdi_tr_gro/sdi
_tr1230 (08.11.2007)

EuroStat8 n.d.
EuroStat (ed.) (no date): Emissionen von Ozonvorläufern durch Straßenverkehr.
http://epp.eurostat.ec.europa.eu/pls/portal/url/page/PGP_QUEEN/PGE_QUEEN_DE
TAIL?screen=detailref&language=de&product=sdi_tr&root=sdi_tr/sdi_tr/sdi_tr_imp/sd
i_tr1300 (08.11.2007)

EuroStat9 n.d.
EuroStat (ed.) (no date): Treibhausgasemissionen durch Verkehr.
http://epp.eurostat.ec.europa.eu/portal/page?_pageid=1996,39140985&_dad=portal&
_schema=PORTAL&screen=detailref&language=de&product=sdi_tr&root=sdi_tr/sdi_t
r/sdi_tr_imp/sdi_tr1400 (08.11.2007)

EuroStat10 n.d.
EuroStat (ed.) (no date): Verkehrstote.
http://epp.eurostat.ec.europa.eu/pls/portal/url/page/PGP_QUEEN/PGE_QUEEN_DE
TAIL?screen=detailref&language=de&product=sdi_tr&root=sdi_tr/sdi_tr/sdi_tr_imp/sd
i_tr1410 (08.11.2007)

EuroStat11 n.d.
EuroStat (ed.) (no date): Verkehrstote, nach Altersklasse.
http://epp.eurostat.ec.europa.eu/pls/portal/url/page/PGP_QUEEN/PGE_QUEEN_DE
TAIL?screen=detailref&language=de&product=sdi_tr&root=sdi_tr/sdi_tr/sdi_tr_imp/sd
i_tr1411 (08.11.2007)

EuroStat12 n.d.
EuroStat (ed.) (no date): Emissionen von NOx durch Straßenfahrzeuge.
http://epp.eurostat.ec.europa.eu/pls/portal/url/page/PGP_QUEEN/PGE_QUEEN_DE
TAIL?screen=detailref&language=de&product=sdi_tr&root=sdi_tr/sdi_tr/sdi_tr_imp/sd
i_tr1420 (08.11.2007)

Ewers/Tegner 2002
Ewers, H.-J./ Tegner, H. (2002): Volkswirtschaftliche Nutzen durch Wettbewerb im
europäischen Air Traffic Management am Beispiel Deutschland. Berlin (Germany).
http://www.wip.tu-berlin.de/typo3/fileadmin/documents/wip-
de/forschung/publikationen/2002/tu-berlin_wip+pspc_ewers+tegner_2002-
studie_airtraffic_management-final_version.pdf (01.01.2008)

GIC 2007
German-Irish Chamber of Industry and Commerce (ed.) (2007): German-Irish
Business. Dublin (Ireland).

Himanen et al 1995
Himanen et al (1995): Evolution of Transport Networks Around the Core Area of
Europe.
In: Banister, D./ Capello, R./ Nijkamp, P.: European Transport and Communication
Networks. Policy evolution and change. Chichester (UK). P. 47 - 67.
Huber 1993
Huber, A. (1993): Wettbewerbsprobleme des grenzüberschreitenden
Schienengüterverkehrs im europäischen Integrationsraum. http://www.ub.uni-
konstanz.de/kops/volltexte/1999/154/pdf/154_1.pdf (12.12.2007)

INE n.d.
Inland Navigation Europe (ed.) (no date): INE - Multimodal Transport Policy. Brussels
(Belgium). http://www.inlandnavigation.org/en/transport/mtp.html (01.01.08)

Max-Planck 1987
Max-Planck-Institut für ausländisches und internationales Privatrecht (ed.) (1987):
Europäische Verkehrspolitik. Tübingen (Germany).

Mehl 2004
Mehl, Matthias (2004): Die Anwendung des Subsidiaritätsprinzips auf dem Gebiet der Europäischen Verkehrspolitik. Zugleich eine Studie über die gemeinschaftliche Rechtsetzungsbefugnis im Verkehrssektor. Frankfurt am Main (Germany).

Meyers1 2007
Meyers Lexikon Online 2.0 (ed.) (2007): Verkehr.
http://lexikon.meyers.de/meyers/Verkehr (14.11.2007)

Meyers2 2007
Meyers Lexikon Online 2.0 (ed.) (2007): Verkehrspolitik.
http://lexikon.meyers.de/meyers/Verkehrspolitik (14.11.2007)

Meyers3 2007
Meyers Lexikon Online 2.0 (ed.) (2007): Nachhaltigkeit.
http://lexikon.meyers.de/meyers/Nachhaltigkeit (14.11.2007)

Nuhn/ Hesse 2006
Nuhn, H./ Hesse, M. (2006): Verkehrsgeographie. Paderborn [u.a.] (Germany).

OECD 2004
OECD (ed.) (2004): OECD/ECMT Transport Research Centre. Conclusions Round Table 132: Transport Infrastructure Investment and Productivity. Paris (France).
http://www.cemt.org/online/conclus/rt132e.pdf (11.11.2007)

OECD 2005
OECD (ed.) (2005): OECD Transport, Figures 2003-05.
http://dx.doi.org/10.1787/353365538624 (11.11.2007)

OECD1 2007
OECD (ed.) (2004): OECD/ECMT Transport Research Centre. Conclusions Round Table 137: Transport, Urban Form and Economic Growth. Berkeley (USA).
http://www.cemt.org/online/conclus/rt137e.pdf (11.11.2007)

OECD2 2007
OECD (ed.) (2007): OECD Factbook 2007 – Economic, environmental and social statistics. Quality of life: Transport – Growth of the motorway network.
http://lysander.sourceoecd.org/vl=2001081/cl=20/nw=1/rpsv/factbook/11-04-01-g01.htm (11.11.2007)

OECD3 2007
OECD (ed.) (2007): OECD Factbook 2007 – Economic, environmental and social statistics. Quality of life: Transport – Road motor vehicles and road fatalities.
http://lysander.sourceoecd.org/vl=2001081/cl=20/nw=1/rpsv/factbook/11-04-02.htm (11.11.2007)

OECD4 2007
OECD (ed.) (2007): OECD Factbook 2007 – Economic, environmental and social statistics. Quality of life: Transport – Road motor vehicles.
http://lysander.sourceoecd.org/vl=2001081/cl=20/nw=1/rpsv/factbook/11-04-02-g01.htm (11.11.2007)

OECD5 2007
OECD (ed.) (2007): OECD Factbook 2007 – Economic, environmental and social statistics. Quality of life: Transport – Road fatalities.
http://lysander.sourceoecd.org/vl=2001081/cl=20/nw=1/rpsv/factbook/11-04-02-g02.htm (11.11.2007)

OECD6 2007
OECD (ed.) (2007): OECD Factbook 2007 – Economic, environmental and social statistics. Quality of life: Transport – Road fatalities.
http://lysander.sourceoecd.org/vl=2001081/cl=20/nw=1/rpsv/factbook/11-04-02-g03.htm (11.11.2007)

OECD7 2007
OECD (ed.) (2007): OECD Factbook 2007 – Economic, environmental and social statistics. Quality of life: Transport – Road network.
http://lysander.sourceoecd.org/vl=2001081/cl=20/nw=1/rpsv/factbook/11-04-01.htm (11.11.2007)

SkySails 2006
SkySails GmbH & Co. KG (ed.) (2006): Förderungen. Hamburg (Germany).
http://skysails.info/index.php?id=99&L=0 (01.01.2008)

Towey 2005
Towey, F. (2005): European Transport Policy – an Irish perspective. Tralee (Ireland).
http://www.kerrycoco.ie/NASC/No%20%205%202005%2003%20Transport-Towey.rtf (11.11.2007)

UNECE et al 2003
UNECE, ECMT, EuroStat (ed.) (2003): Glossary for Transport Statistics. Paris (France). http://www.cemt.org/online/glossaries/glostat3e.pdf (11.11.2007)

UNECE 2007
United Nations Economic Commission for Europe (ed.) (2007): About the UNECE Transport Division. Main activities of the Transport Division.
http://www.unece.org/trans/presentTransDiv.html (11.11.2007)

Van de Voorde/Viegas 1995
In: Banister, D./ Capello, R./ Nijkamp, P. (1995): European Transport and Communication Networks. Policy evolution and change. Chichester (UK). P. 31 - 44.

Weidenfeld 1992
Weidenfeld, W. (1992): Einführung: Verkehrspolitik im Europa von morgen.
In: Button, Kenneth (ed.): Europäische Verkehrspolitik – Wege in die Zukunft. Strategien und Optionen für die Zukunft Europas. Gütersloh (Germany). P. 11 - 26.

Lightning Source UK Ltd.
Milton Keynes UK
UKHW010759200721
387465UK00003B/926